THE
FUNNIEST
JOKE
BOOK
EVER!

PORTABLE
PRESS

THE FUNNIEST JOKE BOOK EVER

Copyright © 2016 Portable Press

Portable Press/The Bathroom Readers' Institute
An imprint of Printers Row Publishing Group
10350 Barnes Canyon Road, Suite 100, San Diego, CA 92121
www.portablepress.com
e-mail: mail@bathroomreader.com

Printers Row Publishing Group is a division of Readerlink Distribution Services, LLC. The Portable Press names and logos are trademarks of Readerlink Distribution Services, LLC.

All correspondence concerning the content of this book should be addressed to Portable Press/The Bathroom Readers' Institute, Editorial Department, at the above address.

Cover and Interior Design by Patrick Merrell

THANK YOU!

*Portable Press sincerely thanks those whose
creative efforts made this book possible.*

Gordon Javna	Jay Newman	Melinda Allman
Kim T. Griswell	Hannah Bingham	Jonathan Lopes
Trina Janssen	Peter Norton	Rusty von Dyl
Brian Boone	Aaron Guzman	Readerlink, LLC

ISBN 978-1-62686-584-6

Printed in USA

Second Printing

20 19 18 17 16   2 3 4 5 6

What do you call a kid captured by a cannibal?

Stu!

What do you get when you cross a bear with a skunk?

Winnie the Pew.

When the moth hit the windshield, what was the last thing to go through its mind?

Its butt!

What do you call a cow with a twitch?

Beef jerky.

What do you call a hippy's wife?

Mississippi.

How does Darth Vader like his toast?

On the dark side!

Q&A JOKES

If we breathe oxygen during the day, what do we breathe at night?

Nightrogen.

What's the hardest thing about learning to skate?

The ground!

What kind of bagel can fly?

A plain bagel.

Why shouldn't you write with a broken pencil?

It's pointless.

Why couldn't the gnome pay his rent?

He was a little short.

What do you call a prehistoric pig?

Jurassic pork!

Why is it dangerous to do math in the jungle?

Because if you add 4 and 4, you get ate.

Why did dinosaurs walk so slowly?

Because running shoes hadn't been invented yet.

Why did the little strawberry cry?

Her mom and dad were in a jam.

Why did the rooster cross the road?

It was the chicken's day off.

What do you call a fake noodle?

An impasta.

Why don't zombies eat clowns?

They taste funny!

What do you give to a sick lemon?

Lemon aid.

Who makes the best exploding underwear?

Fruit of the Boom!

What do you call a grizzly bear caught in a rain shower?

A drizzly bear.

What kind of songs are balloons afraid of?

Pop songs!

What is every magician's favorite candy bar?

Twix.

What's white, furry, and
shaped like a tooth?

A molar bear.

Did you hear about the computer
program created by a chicken?

All you do is point and cluck.

What did the alpaca say when she
was kicked off the farm?

Alpaca my bags!

What's the most important rule for
doing science experiments?

Never lick the spoon.

What would bears be without bees?

Ears!

What do you give a seasick monster?

Plenty of room!

Why did the cowboy ride the bull?

It was too heavy to carry.

Which Great Lake do ghosts like best?

Lake Eerie.

Why do the French eat snails?

Because they don't like fast food.

How did the frozen chicken cross the road?

In a shopping bag.

What do you call a rabbit with fleas?

Bugs Bunny.

If athletes get athlete's feet, what do astronauts get?

Missile toe!

Why can't you hear a pterodactyl going to the bathroom?

Because the "p" is silent.

**What do you get when you cross
a goat with a squid?**

Billy the Squid.

**Have you heard the joke
about the peach?**

It's pitiful.

**Which bird can hold three gallons
of water in its bill?**

The pelican.

**Where does Spiderman go for
medical advice?**

Web MD.

Why was the potato alone at the party?

It got there oily.

What's the best time to visit the dentist?

Tooth-hurty!

Which state needs a handkerchief?

Mass-ACHOO!-setts.

Why do fish choirs always sing off-key?

Because you can't tuna fish.

What kind of undies do clouds wear?

Thunderwear!

Did you hear about the frog
that was illegally parked?

It got toad.

Why did the toilet paper
roll down the hill?

To get to the bottom.

If April showers bring May flowers,
what do May flowers bring?

Pilgrims!

What do you call a motorcycle with a
good sense of humor?

A Yamahahaha.

Q&A JOKES

**Why did the kid leave his
piggy bank outside?**

He expected some change
in the weather.

**Why didn't the teddy bear
eat his oatmeal?**

He was already stuffed!

What kind of books do skunks read?

Best-smellers.

Why do vampires brush their teeth?

To prevent bat breath.

**Where do baby ghosts
spend their days?**

At day-scare centers.

What do you call a sleeping T. rex?

A dino-snore!

**Why did the cantaloupe jump
into the lake?**

It wanted to be a watermelon.

Why did the belt get arrested?

It held up a pair of pants.

Why are batteries always sad?

Because they're never included.

How can you fall off a 100-foot ladder without getting hurt?

Easy! Fall from the bottom rung.

How is Facebook like a refrigerator?

Because every few minutes you open it to see if there's anything good in it.

If Pilgrims were alive today, what would they be most famous for?

Their age!

**What's the best day to go
to the beach?**

Sun-day.

**What do baby sweet potatoes
wear to bed?**

Their yammies!

**What's green, has big eyes, and is
hard to see through?**

Kermit the Fog.

What kind of car does a farmer drive?

A corn-vertible.

**Where do you send a shoe
in the summer?**

Boot camp!

**Why were early days of history called
the Dark Ages?**

Because there were so many knights.

**What did one car muffler say to the
other car muffler?**

"Boy, am I exhausted!"

**What should you shout if you swim into
kelp and get caught in it?**

"Kelp!"

What lives at the bottom of the ocean and is popular on Easter?

Oyster eggs.

What do you say to a hitchhiking angel?

"Harp in!"

How do you make antifreeze?

Steal her blanket.

What has a big mouth but can't talk?

A jar.

What's red and smells like blue paint?

Red paint.

Which kind of dog can jump higher than a building?

Any dog. Buildings can't jump.

What looks like half of a cat?

The other half.

**What do cats like to eat
for dessert?**

Mice cream.

**What should you know before
you teach a dog a trick?**

More than the dog!

Which movie is a feline favorite?

The Sound of Mew-sic.

**Why can dogs scratch whenever
they want to?**

They live in a flea country.

What did the alien say to the cat?

Take me to your litter!

Will: If you want to find your dog, you should put an ad in the paper.

Bill: Don't be silly. Fido can't read!

Which cats make the best bowlers?

Alley cats.

Why are dogs such terrible dancers?

They have two left feet.

How do you spell mousetrap using three letters? C-A-T!

What did the dog say when it sat
on the sandpaper?

Ruff.

Cat: What smells the most in
a garbage dump?

Rat: The nose.

Which household cleaner do
Dalmatians fear most?

Spot remover.

What do you call a guy who's been
attacked by a cat?

Claude!

Why did the dog say "Meow!"?

He was trying to learn
a second language.

What's a cat's favorite song?

Three Blind Mice.

**What do you get when you cross
a dog and a dandelion?**

A collie-flower.

**Which game do cats like to
play with mice?**

Catch!

Where do dogs go when their tails fall off?

The retail store.

How do cats end a fight?

They hiss and make up.

What did the Dalmatian say after eating?

That hit the spots!

What's smarter than a talking cat?

A spelling bee.

How do fleas get from one dog
to another dog?

By itch-hiking.

Why was the kitten in such a
bad mood?

She needed a catnap.

Why did the dog cross the road...twice?

To fetch a boomerang!

What do cats like to put in their milk?

Mice cubes.

Which breed of dog loves taking baths?

Shampoodles!

Why do cats scratch themselves?

Because no one else knows
where the itch is.

How do you keep a dog from smelling?

Put a clothespin on its nose.

Why can't cats finish watching DVDs?

They can't resist pressing
the "paws" button.

What did one flea say to the other flea when they walked out of the movie?

Shall we walk or take the dog?

What do you call a giant pile of cats?

A meowtain.

What do sheep dogs turn into every summer?

Hot dogs!

Why are cats terrible story tellers?

They only have one tail.

Why do dogs run around in circles?

It's hard to run around in squares.

What breakfast cereal do cats like best?

Mice Krispies!

Why did the Dachshund bite his trainer's ankle?

He couldn't reach any higher.

What do you call a cat that just swallowed a duck?

A duck filled fatty puss.

When is a bloodhound dumb?

When it has no scents.

Why do cats climb trees?

Because they don't have ladders.

Why did the terrier have splinters in his tongue?

He kept eating table scraps.

When is it bad luck to have a black cat cross your path?

When you're a mouse!

DOGS & CATS

Which holiday do dogs like best?

Howl-o-ween.

What do you get if you cross a rabbit with two cats?

Hare! Kitty kitty!

Which dogs make the best teachers?

Grade Danes.

How can you tell if a cat burglar has been in your house?

Your cat is missing.

3

YUM YUKS!

What does Godzilla eat at a restaurant?

The restaurant!

Why couldn't the bagel escape?

It was covered with lox.

YUM YUKS

**What kind of candy do you
eat on the playground?**

Recess Pieces.

Why did the beet turn red?

It saw the salad dressing.

Did you hear about the crazy pancake?

He just flipped!

**What is Peter Pan's favorite
fast food restaurant?**

Wendy'n.

Who makes shoes for fruit?

A peach cobbler.

How do you fix a broken pizza?

With tomato paste.

Who writes nursery rhymes and squeezes oranges?

Mother Juice.

Kid: Waiter! There's a bee in my soup.

Waiter: Of course. You ordered alphabet soup.

What was the snowman's favorite cereal?

Frosted Flakes.

Which food can you eat in the bathroom?

Showerkraut.

What's green, has 22 legs, and plays football?

The Green Bay Pickles.

Why did the pie go to the dentist?

It needed a filling.

What's brown, wrinkled, and lives
in a tower?

The Lunch Bag of Notre Dame.

What do you get when you cross a pig
and a centipede?

Bacon and legs.

Why did the baker stop making
doughnuts?

He was tired of the hole business.

Did you hear about the guy who
drank food coloring?

He dyed a little inside.

YUM YUKS

What starts with a T, ends with a T, and is full of T?

A teapot.

What does the ocean eat for breakfast?

Boatmeal.

Why are tightrope walkers so healthy?

They always eat a balanced diet.

What do computers snack on?

Microchips.

What do you call a baby potato?

A small fry.

What did the baby corn say to the mama corn?

Where's Popcorn?

Why did the cookie visit the doctor?

It was feeling crummy.

What do you call a potato at a football game?

A spec-tater!

What was the anteater's favorite pizza topping?

Antchovies!

What do you get when you cross a bee with chopped meat?

Humburger.

What did the banana do when it saw a horde of hungry monkeys?

Split.

Why did the kid stare at frozen orange juice can all day?

Because the label said "concentrate."

What does a nosy pepper do?

Gets jalapeño business.

A kid walks into a soda shop with a slab of asphalt under his arm and says, "A root beer please, and one for the road."

Which potato makes the best detective?

One whose eyes are peeled.

What did the hot dog say when it won the race?

"I'm a weiner!"

What happens when the chef goes on strike?

You have a cook-out.

What does a panda fry his bamboo in?

A pan...duh!

What did the frog order at McDonald's?

Flies and a diet croak.

Dad: Sorry, son, but I only know how to make two dishes, meat loaf and apple pie.

Son: Which one is this?

Why did the potato cross the road?

It saw a fork up ahead.

Best Cookbook: *Hot Dog* **by Frank Furter**

YUM YUKS

**What did one plate say to
the other plate?**

Lunch is on me!

What kind of nut doesn't have a shell?

A doughnut.

**Did you hear the joke about the
pepperoni pizza?**

Never mind. It's way too cheesy.

**What kind of ice cream is
bad at tennis?**

Soft serve.

YUM YUKS

Which day do eggs hate?

Fry-day.

Which food stays hot in the fridge?

Hot dogs.

What do ghosts eat for lunch?

Boo-loney sandwiches.

What do you call a stolen yam?

A hot potato.

What do you call a small hot dog?

A teenie weenie!

How do you make soup into gold?

Add 14 carrots.

What does a snowman put in his coffee?

Cold cream.

Why was the salad naked?

The waitress forgot the dressing.

Why don't tomatoes like to box?

They get beat to a pulp.

What is a tree's favorite drink?

Root beer.

When does hot chocolate cause a stabbing pain in the eye?

When you forget to take out the spoon!

Where does Santa go to buy potatoes?

Idaho-ho-ho!

Why did the kid have string beans stuck up his nose?

He wasn't eating properly.

It was so hot...

...the cornfield popped,

...the cows gave evaporated milk,

..the grapes turned to raisins, and

...the chickens laid hardboiled eggs!

4

What do you call a stupid pirate?

The pillage idiot.

Why couldn't the pirate play cards?

He was sitting on the deck!

PIRATE JOKES

Why did the pirate walk the plank?

Because he couldn't afford a dog.

Which pirate makes the best clam chowder?

Captain Cook!

Why did the pirate put a chicken on top of his treasure chest?

Because eggs mark the spot.

What did the pirate say when his wooden leg got stuck in a snow bank?

"Shiver me timbers!"

PIRATE JOKES

**Why wouldn't the pirate fight
the octopus?**

It was too well-armed.

What type of socks do pirates wear?

Arrrrrgyle.

Why did the pirate buy an eye patch?

He couldn't afford an iPhone.

**Why didn't the pirate take a bath
before he walked the plank?**

He knew he would just wash up on
shore later.

What did the pirate say on his 80th birthday?

"Aye, matey!"

Where do pirate ships go when they're sick?

To the dock.

Where can you find a pirate who has lost his wooden legs?

Right where you left him.

What's a pirates favorite vegetable?

Arrrrrtichoke

First Mate: Feeding the prisoners to the sharks isn't any fun.

Captain: It is for the sharks!

What happened when the red pirate ship sank in the Black Sea?

The crew was marooned.

Why are pirates called pirates?

Cause they just arrrrr!

Why do pirate captains always sing tenor?

They're the only ones who can hit the high C's.

PIRATE JOKES

Whore did the pirate leave his keys?

Off the coast of Florida.

**What do you call a pirate with
two eyes and two legs?**

Rookie.

**What has eight arms, eight legs,
and eight eyes?**

Eight pirates.

**Where did the one-legged pirate go
for breakfast?**

IHOP.

What is the pirate's favorite letter in the alphabet?

X...That's where the treasure is.

How much do pirates pay for their earrings?

A buck an ear (buccaneer).

Did you hear about the new *Pirates of the Caribbean* movie?

It was rated Ar-r-r-r!

Why was it rated Ar-r-r-r?

Too much booty!

PIRATE JOKES

What do you call a pirate droid?

Arrrrr2-D2

What happened to the pirate who couldn't pee?

He became irate.

What's the difference between a jeweler and the captain of a ship?

One sees the watches and the other watches the seas.

How does a pirate know when the sea is friendly?

It waves.

5

FAIRY FUNNY!

Who helped Fisherella get to the ball?

Her fairy Codmother.

Why did Robin Hood steal money from the rich?

Because the poor didn't have any.

Who was the fattest knight at King Arthur's Round Table?

Sir Cumference.

What do you call a princess who falls down on the ice?

Slipping Beauty.

On which side of the house did Jack grow the beanstalk?

The outside.

Why is Tinkerbell always flying around?

Because she lives in Neverland.

Why did Cinderella get kicked off the soccer team?

She kept running away from the ball.

First Dragon: Am I too late for dinner?

Second Dragon: Yes. Everyone's eaten.

Who weighs two tons and went to the ball wearing glass slippers?

Cinderelephant.

Why did Robin Hood's men hate living in Sherwood Forest?

It only had one Little John.

**Who carves wooden figures and lives
under the sea?**

The Whittle Mermaid.

**What do you get if you cross Tinkerbell
with a werewolf?**

A hairy fairy.

**What do you get if you cross a hairy
fairy with a monster?**

A scary hairy fairy.

**What laundry detergent does
the Little Mermaid use?**

Tide.

Optician: Have your eyes ever been checked?

Ogre: No. They've always been red.

Why does Snow White treat all of the dwarves equally?

Because she's the fairest of all.

How did Jack know how many beans his cow was worth?

He used a cowculator.

Fairyland Bestsellers:

How to Cook Crocodile by Stu Potts

Aladdin's Lamp: The Inside Story by A. Genie

Who Killed Captain Hook? by Howard I. Know

FAIRY TALE JOKES

Why can't Goldilocks sleep?

Night-bears!

Why did the Little Mermaid blush?

She saw the ship's bottom!

Why did Rapunzel go to parties?

She liked to let her hair down!

How is Prince Charming like a book?

He has a lot of pages.

What do you call a wee cottage?

A gnome home.

What is Humpty Dumpty's least favorite season?

Fall.

Who stole the soap from the Three Bears' bathroom?

The robber ducky.

What did Peter Pan say when he saw the tornado?

Look! It's Wendy.

Why didn't the Fairy Godmother laugh at Cinderella's jokes?

They weren't fairy funny.

FAIRY TALE JOKES

Where does Robin Hood like to shop?

At Target.

Who's the smartest fairy in Neverland?

Thinkerbell.

What do you call a fairy that won't bathe?

Stinkerbell.

Why is the ocean floor so sandy?

There are never enough mermaids

Why is the Tooth Fairy so smart?

She's collected a lot of wisdom teeth.

6

Knock-knock!

Who's there?

Comma.

Comma who?

Comma little closer and I'll tell you!

Knock-knock!

Who's there?

Interrupting chicken.

Interrupting chick—

HEY! WANNA CROSS THE ROAD?

Knock-knock!

Who's there?

Dishes.

Dishes who?

Dishes the way I talk since I lost my two front teeth!

Knock-knock!

Who's there?

Ya.

Ya who?

Sorry. I prefer Google.

Knock-knock!
Who's there?
Amos.
Amos who?
A mosquito bit me.

Knock-knock!
Who's there?
Andy.
Andy who?
Andy bit me again!

Knock-knock!
Who's there?
Omelette.
Omelette who?
Omelette smarter than I look.

Why did the duck cross the road?

To get to your house.

Knock-knock!

Who's there?

The duck!

Knock-knock!

Who's there?

Stan.

Stan who?

Stan back! I'm going to kick the door down.

M-O-O...!

Knock-Knock!

Who's there?

Time-traveling cow.

Knock-knock!

Who's there?

Deluxe.

Deluxe who?

Deluxe-smith. I'm here to fix de lock.

Knock-knock!

Who's there?

Ida.

Ida who?

Ida called first but my cell phone died.

Knock-knock!

Who's there?

Howdy!

Howdy who?

Howdy do that?

Knock-knock!

Who's there?

Euripides.

Euripides who?

Euripides pants you buy me new ones.

Knock-knock!

Who's there?

Cows go.

Cows go who?

No, silly! Cows go "MOO"!

Knock-knock!

Who's there?

Interrupting Zombie.

Interrupting Zom—

"BRAAAINS!"

Knock-knock!
Who's there?
Europe.
Europe who?
What? No, you're a poo!

Knock-knock!
Who's there?
Althea.
Althea who?
Althea later alligator!

Knock-knock!
Who's there?
Dare.
Dare who?
Dare must be some mistake!

Knock-knock!

Who's there?

Dozen.

Dozen who?

Dozen anyone care that I'm stuck outside in the cold?

Knock-knock!

Who's there?

Topeka.

Topeka who?

Why do you like Topeka your nose?

Knock-knock!

Who's there?

Pig.

Pig who?

Pig me up after school, please!

Knock-knock!
Who's there?
Kenya.
Kenya who?
Kenya come out and play after dinner?

Knock-knock!
Who's there?
Will Hugh.
Will Hugh who?
Will Hugh toss that ball back over the fence?

Knock-knock!
Who's there?
Zeno.
Zeno who?
Zeno evil. Hear no evil.

Knock-knock!

Who's there?

My panther.

My panther who?

My panther falling down.

Knock-knock!

Who's there?

Ooze.

Ooze who?

Ooze afraid of the Big Bad Wolf?

Knock-knock!

Who's there?

Weird.

Weird who?

Weird you hide the chocolate?

Knock-knock!

Who's there?

Yoda.

Yoda who?

Yoda weirdest person I know.

Knock-knock!

Who's there?

Skip.

Skip who?

Just skip it. I'll go next door.

Knock-knock!

Who's there?

Tubby.

Tubby who?

**Tubby or not Tubby?
That is the question.**

Knock-knock!
Who's there?
I am.
I am who?
You mean you don't know?

Knock-knock!
Who's there?
Wooden.
Wooden who?
Wooden you like to know!

Knock-knock!
Who's there?
Saul.
Saul who?
Saul there is, there ain't no more!

7

ELEPHANTS

Why do elephants wear tennies?

Because ninies are too small and
elevenies are too big!

What is big and gray and blue?

An elephant holding its breath.

**Why did the elephant
change his socks?**

Because they were dirty.

Why do elephants have a trunk?

They would look silly carrying a hatbox.

**What did the worm say after he crawled
under the elephant's foot?**

I'll never have the guts to
do that again!

**What's worse than an elephant with
no shirt on?**

A hippo-bottomless.

What time is it when an elephant sits on the fence?

Time to get a new fence.

What time is it when an elephant sits on an electric fence?

Time to get a new elephant!

Why do elephants paint their toenails red, yellow, orange, green, and brown?

So they can hide in a bag of M&Ms.

Why didn't the elephant wear pajamas at camp?

He forgot to pack his trunk.

ELEPHANT JOKES

Why do ducks have webbed feet?

To stamp out forest fires.

Where do elephants with zits go?

To the pachydermatologist.

Why do elephants have flat feet?

To stamp out flaming ducks!

Which elephants live in the Arctic?

The cold ones.

What's big, gray, and lives in Scotland?

The Loch Ness Elephant.

ELEPHANT JOKES

What kind of elephants live at the North Pole?

Cold ones.

What do you get when you cross an elephant with peanut butter?

An elephant that sticks to the roof of your mouth.

Why are elephants large, gray, and wrinkled?

If they were small, round, and white, they'd be aspirins.

Why can't you take an elephant to school?

It won't fit in your backpack.

ELEPHANT JOKES

How do you tell an elephant from
a dozen eggs?

If you don't know, I'll send someone
else to the store.

Why do elephants walk sideways
through grass?

To trip the field mice.

What's gray and has four legs
and a trunk?

A mouse going on vacation.

How do you get down from an
elephant?

You don't. You get down from a duck.

What do you call an elephant that doesn't matter?

An irrelephant.

What goes "thump, thump, thump, squish"?

An elephant with one wet sneaker.

What do you get if you drop an elephant on a baby butterfly?

A splatterpillar.

How can you tell when there are three elephants in the bathtub with you?

You count them!

ELEPHANT JOKES

What do you call an elephant that never takes a bath?

A smellyphant.

Why did the elephant paint his toenails different colors?

To hide in the jelly bean jar.

Have you ever found an elephant in a jelly bean jar?

See? It works.

Who started the elephant jokes?

That's what the elephants want to know.

When does a baby elephant look like a cute little bunny?

When she's wearing a cute little bunny suit.

What do you do with old bowling balls?

Give them to elephants to use as marbles.

Why do elephants wear sandals?

So they don't sink in the sand.

Why do ostriches stick their head in the sand?

To look for the elephants who forgot to wear their sandals.

Why do elephants have big ears?

To keep their sunglasses from falling off.

Why do elephants wear sunglasses?

So Tarzan doesn't recognize them.

What did Tarzan say when he saw a herd of elephants running through the jungle?

Nothing. He didn't recognize them with their sunglasses on.

Why do elephants have wrinkled knees?

They tie their tennis shoes too tight.

8

HUMDINGERS

What did the drummer get on his IQ test?

Saliva.

Who is the wasp's favorite composer?

Bee-thoven.

Did you hear about the cobra that hid in the tuba?

He was a real snake in the brass.

What has lots of keys but can't open doors?

A piano.

Why do bagpipers march when they play?

To get away from the noise.

Why did the rock star bring a pencil on stage?

He wanted to draw a big crowd.

What's the difference between an accordion and an onion?

No one cries when you chop up an accordion.

Did you hear about the band called 1023 Megabytes?

They were on their way to a gig.

What is the squirrel's favorite opera?

The Nutcracker.

What is the rabbit's favorite music?

Hip-hop!

What's Beethoven's favorite fruit?

Ba-na-na-na!!!

Why was the pop star get arrested?

She got in treble!

What song to vampires hates?

You are my sunshine.

What do you call a musical pickle?

A piccolo.

What's big and gray with horns?

An elephant marching band.

**Why did the school band have
such bad manners?**

It didn't know how to conduct itself.

Why are pop stars so cool?

They have millions of fans.

Why did Mozart hate chickens?

They're always running around going
"Bach! Bach! Bach!"

**How do you get your dad
to drive really fast?**

Put your drums in the middle of the road.

HUMDINGERS

Why did the chicken cross the road?

To get away from the oboe recital.

How do you clean a tuba?

With a tuba toothpaste.

Why don't guitarists work?

They only know how to play.

Why did the punk rocker cross the road?

He was stapled to a chicken.

Why was the guitar mad?

It was tired of being picked on.

What kind of paper makes music?

Rapping paper!

Why did the pianist bang the side of his head against the keyboard?

He was playing by ear.

Where do vampire violinists go for vacation?

The Vile Inn.

What's the most musical part of a turkey?

The drumstick.

HUMDINGERS

What was stolen from the music store?

The lute!

How do you make a bandstand?

Take away their chairs!

Why do hummingbirds hum?

They forgot the words.

Why shouldn't kids go to the symphony?

Too much sax and violins.

What kind of band doesn't play music?

A rubber band.

9

SPACE CASE

When does the Moon stop eating?

When it's full.

What tastes better, a comet or an asteroid?

An asteroid, because it's meteor!

Why does E.T. have such big eyes?

He saw his phone bill.

**Which astronaut wears
the biggest helmet?**

The one with the biggest head.

How do you serve aliens dinner?

On flying saucers.

Favorite Space Book:
Full Moon by Seymour Buns

**How do astronauts keep warm on the
International Space Station?**

They turn up the space heater.

How do meteors stay clean?

They shower!

What does an astronaut wear to bed?

Space jammies.

What did the astronomer see at the center of Jupiter?

The letter "i".

What's the difference between E.T. and a teenager?

E.T. actually phoned home.

Why did the space restaurant close down?

It lacked atmosphere.

What do you get when you cross a kangaroo with an alien?

A Mars-upial.

Did you hear about the astronaut who broke the law of gravity?

She got a suspended sentence.

Why was the Moon acting so loony?

It was going through a phase.

**How does the universe
hold up its pants?**

With an asteroid belt.

**What do stars do when they
want a snack?**

Take a bite out of the Milky Way.

**How do you throw the best party in
the Solar System?**

You planet.

What did the astronaut cook for lunch?

An unidentified frying object.

SPACE JOKES

How do you get an astronaut's baby
to fall asleep?

You rocket.

What is Han Solo's favorite
restaurant?

Jabba the Pizza Hutt.

Captain Kirk: "Our next mission
takes us to the Sun."

Scotty: "We canna do it, Captain!
The Sun is far too hot."

Captain Kirk: "Don't worry, Mr. Scott.
We'll land at night."

What kind of songs do astronauts like?

Neptunes!

SPACE JOKES

What do you call a UFO with a leak?

A crying saucer.

What did the alien say to the garden?

Take me to your weeder.

How do Martians count to 13?

On their fingers.

Teacher: Which is closer, China or the Moon?

Kid: Duh...the Moon. You can't see China from here.

What was the alien's favorite taco filling?

Human beans.

Why did the chicken cross the galaxy?

To boldly go where no chicken
had gone before.

**Luke: I hear Dracula will be staring
in the next Star Wars movie.**

Yoda: Really? What's it called?

Luke: The Vampire Strikes Back.

**What did the ones say to the twos
and threes?**

"May the fours be with you!"

What kind of life was found on Pluto?

Fleas.

When can't you visit the Moon?

When it's full.

On which planet did the space probe crash?

Splaturn!

What do you get when you cross a toad with the Sun?

Star warts.

Where do otters come from?

Otter space.

An astronaut's favorite fish: stardines.

What did E.T.'s mom say when he returned home?

"Where on Earth have you been!"

Why don't Martians drown in hot chocolate?

They sit on the Mars-mallows.

How does the Moon cut his hair when the Sun gets in the way?

Eclipse it.

Why did the space shuttle pilot eat beans every day?

He didn't want to run out of gas.

10

ONE-LINERS

Whatever you do, always give 100%.
Unless you're donating blood.

A kid goes to the store to buy some
toilet paper. The clerk asks him what
color he'd like. "White," says the kid.
"I'll color it myself!"

My friend told me an onion is the only food that makes you cry, so I threw a coconut at his face.

There's only one good thing about getting hit in the head with a can of Coke. It's a soft drink.

A pessimist's blood-type is always B-negative.

Whoever invented knock-knock jokes should get a no-bell prize.

A magician was walking down the street and turned into a grocery store.

The time traveler was still hungry after his last bite, so he went back four seconds.

What is the difference between ignorance and apathy? I don't know, and I don't care.

A cowboy, a clown, and a fireman walk into a bar. Ow!

I was addicted to the Hokey Pokey... but I turned myself around. Isn't that what it's all about?

The wig thief struck again last night. Police are combing the area.

Jokes about german sausages
are the wurst.

When fish are in schools, they
sometimes take debate.

A dog gave birth to puppies in the park
and was cited for littering.

Two silk worms had a race.
They ended up in a tie.

My dog can do magic tricks. It's a
labracadabrador.

I was struggling to figure out how
lightning works, then it struck me.

Parallel lines have so much in common.
It's a shame they'll never meet.

If Iron Man and the Silver Surfer
teamed up, they would be alloys.

Just went to an emotional wedding...
even the cake was in tiers.

Two antennae decided to get married.
The ceremony was dull, but the
reception was great!

Living on Earth might be expensive,
but at least you get a free trip
around the Sun every year.

I know a lot of jokes about unemployed people, but none of them work.

Why do we cook bacon
and bake cookies?

A black hole is a tunnel at the end of the light.

Time flies...when you throw your alarm clock across the room.

A rancher had 196 cows in his field, but when he rounded them up he had 200.

Taller kids always sleep longer.

ONE-LINERS

I was up all night wondering where the Sun had gone...then it dawned on me.

I would go rock climbing if I were a little boulder.

I used to have a fear of hurdles, but I got over it.

If a boomerang always comes back to you, why throw it in the first place?

Dad gave me a bat for my birthday but the first time I tried to play with it, it flew away.

Dry erase boards are remarkable.

Just wrote a song about a tortilla.
Actually, it was more of a wrap.

**Always keep a smile on your face. It
looks silly anywhere else on your body.**

Silence is golden. Duct tape is silver.

**Two wrongs don't make a right...but
two Wright's did make an airplane!**

To the guy who invented zero:
Thanks for nothing!

11

ANIMAL ANTICS

What kind of key opens a banana?

A monkey.

What did the pig say on the hottest day of summer?

"I'm bacon!"

ANIMAL ANTICS

Why do seagulls fly over the sea?

Because if they flew over the bay
they'd be bagels.

What do you do with a Blue Whale?

Cheer it up!

What do you call a pig who knows karate?

Pork chop.

What do cows read in the morning?

Moospapers.

What clucks and points north?

A magnetic chicken.

ANIMAL ANTICS

What do you call a flying skunk?

A smelly-copter.

What do you call a sheep with no legs?

A cloud.

**Why were the owl parents worried
about their son?**

Because he didn't seem to give a hoot
about anything.

**What's the difference between a cow
and a doughnut?**

It's a lot harder to dunk a cow
in a cup of coffee.

Why did the cow jump over the moon?

The farmer had cold hands.

Why are frogs so happy?

They eat what bugs them.

What's the strongest bird?

The crane.

What has six eyes but can't see?

Three blind mice.

What do you call a sleeping bull?

A bulldozer.

ANIMAL ANTICS

How does a pig get to the hospital?

In a hambulance.

What does a spider bride wear?

A webbing dress.

Why did the canary fail his test?

He was caught tweeting.

Why was the little ant so confused?

Because all of his Uncles were ants.

Why did the rhino were red sneakers?

Because the blue ones were dirty.

ANIMAL ANTICS

Why do seals prefer swimming in salt water?

Because pepper water makes them sneeze.

Where do cows go for first dates?

To the moo-vies.

What's orange, has stripes, and is red all over?

A tiger with a sunburn.

What do you get if you cross a parrot with a shark?

A bird that will talk your ear off.

How is a turtle like a brick?

Neither one can play the trumpet.

How do you make a milkshake?

Give a cow a pogo stick.

Why do turkeys gobble?

They never learned table manners.

Why do skunks like Valentine's Day?

They're very scent-imental.

How do ducklings escapes their shells?

They eggs-it.

ANIMAL ANTICS

Why did the chicken cross the road?

The light was green.

**Why did the bubble gum
cross the road?**

Because it was stuck to
the chicken's foot.

**What looks like a snake, swims,
and honks?**

An automob-eel.

**Why couldn't the leopard escape
from the zoo?**

He was always spotted.

What do you get if you cross a canary with a 20-foot snake?

A sing-a-long.

Why don't you ever see hippos hiding in trees?

Because they're very good at it.

What did the chicken say when it laid a square egg?

Ouch!

What do you call a bear with no teeth?

A gummy bear.

ANIMAL ANTICS

What's the difference between bird flu and swine flu?

For bird flu, you need tweetment. For swine flu, you need oinkment.

What do you call a man with 50 rabbits under his coat?

Warren.

What do you get when you cross a cow and a duck?

Milk and quackers.

What's a firefly's life motto?

Always look on the bright side.

ANIMAL ANTICS

What do you call a dinosaur wearing high heels?

A My-feet-are-saurus.

Which dinosaur had the biggest vocabulary?

A Thesaurus.

What do you call a paranoid dinosaur?

A Do-you-think-he-saurus?

How do you dress for a dinosaur party?

In a suit of armor.

Why don't dinosaurs talk?

Because they're all dead!

What's the biggest moth in the world?

A mammoth.

How can you tell if a dinosaur is a vegetarian or a meat-eater?

Lay down on a plate and see what happens.

Why was T. rex afraid to visit the library?

His books were 60 million years overdue.

What do you call the dumbest fish in school?

Dinner.

Why did the marsupial from Australia get fired from his job?

Because he wasn't koala-fied.

Why did the cowboy buy a dachshund?

Because someone told him to get a long little doggy.

Why did the cow cross the road?

To get to the udder side.

ANIMAL ANTICS

How do you keep geese from speeding?

Goose bumps.

What did the buffalo say to his son when he left for school?

Bison!

What kind of monkey likes potato chips?

A chipmunk.

What do you call a sheep covered in chocolate?

A candy baa.

ANIMAL ANTICS

What do you call a girl with a frog on her head?

Lily.

Why shouldn't you play poker in the Savannah?

Too many cheetahs.

What's black and white, black and white, and black and white?

A panda rolling down a hill.

What do you call a sheep that dances gracefully?

A baaaaaalerina.

What do you call a cow with four legs?

A cow.

How do pigs communicate with
each other?

Swine language.

How do ants keep warm in the winter?

ANTifreeze.

What do you call a fly with no wings?

A walk!

Who's a boar's favorite painter?

Pig-casso.

ANIMAL ANTICS

What's big, gray, and wrinkly, and goes around in circles?

A rhinoceros in a revolving door.

What do frogs wear in the summer?

Open toad shoes.

Why do pigs have the best writing instruments?

Because their pens never run out of oink.

Why did the chicken cross the schoolyard?

To get to the other slide!